Words From the Soul

Angie Lindsey

BookLeaf Publishing

Presentation by *BookLeaf Publishing*

Web: www.bookleafpub.com

E-mail: info@bookleafpub.com

ISBN: 9789357215978

First edition 2023

DEDICATION

I dedicate this book of poetry to my mother, Lela Drinkard, because without her faith and guidance, and her belief in me, it would have never been possible.

ACKNOWLEDGEMENT

First, I would like to acknowledge God, for pulling me out of my darkest times, whenever I would get lost. He has never left me, nor forsaken me.

Second, I would like to give thanks to all of the people in my life that cause me heartache, and trauma; because without those battles I had to fight, I wouldn't have the great content that I have.

Third, I would like to thank BookLeaf Publishing for this great opportunity.

PREFACE

I have been hurt and betrayed, lied to, cheated on, and I'm yet to cave. I have dealt with the narcissistic abuse, physical, mental, and emotional. So, believe me when I tell you, there isn't anything that I can't handle. I've been the bad guy in someone else's story so they could save face, I've walked through hell for others, so they could have a safe place, so believe me when I tell you, because this is my truth, there's not much you could do to me that I haven't already been through.

My inspiration for this book is to let others know they are not alone in their pain.

The Storm

As I stand in the storm and watch it rage, I feel a
strange connection,
it mirrors the one inside of me, this pain caused by
rejection.
It's dark and cold, and as the rain slashes across my
face,
I feel the loss and loneliness, ripping through my
heart, now a hollow place.
And as the wind whips through the trees, the pain
of losing him, cripples me.
The deafening sound of my soul being torn cannot
be heard, as I fall to my knees.
I sit there with my head hung down, letting the pain
wash over me.
I feel my tears as they drip to the ground.
The thunder vibrates through my soul, and as the
storm rages on,
I feel a hopelessness I cannot control.
The lightning strikes across the sky, and I wonder
how I can feel this much pain and
not die.
Death doesn't want me, so it seems, I'll be living
this nightmare, awake and not in my dreams.

Anger

I sat with my anger far longer than I intended to.
I let it engulf my life, I became one with it.
I needed to know more about this identikit.
Where it came from, how to deal with it.
Sitting their face to face with anger, she said she wasn't here to steal my life,
she wasn't a thief, and her real name, is not anger, but grief.
She broke my heart when she forced me to see,
all of the tragic past memories.
She tore them up, and through them in the air,
she fanned them away without a care.
I knew in that moment I had to let them go,
because only memories like that,
would cause more sorrow.

He looks at me

He looks at me and sees the girl I used to be.
I have trouble remembering her or remembering the girl I used to be.
I've buried her, so very deep.
She was full of emotions, fire and passion, and when he looked at me, I felt her spark.
I felt her stir. She wanted to be set free, she recognized her twin flame.
He is her other half.
I pushed her back down and told her no. You are from the past.
I'm so different now than what he expects to see,
I've given up,
and surrendered to life's cruelty.
She may spark, but I'm not sure there will ever be a flame, I extinguished it when I was drenched in pain.

ANXIETY and DEPRESSION

This life is too much, I can't get out of this bed, I had all this negativity,
swirling through my head.
Depression and Anxiety hitting at its worst, today might be the day,
I need all of these thoughts to just disperse.
I'm damned if I do and damned if I don't, I would ask someone to care,
but I know they won't.
I live in a nightmare, I can't seem to escape, I'm walking on glass, just praying it
doesn't break.
Anxiety and Depression is a losing game, I'm tired of feeling this way,
and if you could understand, you'd feel the same.

INSOMNIA

You to know what it's like to be me?
I'm 38 hours in with no sleep.
My head is pounding, my eyes ache, muscles are throbbing,
I'm exhausted, but somehow, I'm still awake.
I want to hang my head and just cry, but I can't even do that,
because there's no tears, and I don't know why.
My mind doesn't shut off, and my body won't relax, all I can do is pray,
Please God let this end soon, just let me collapse!

THEY BROKE ME

Who was I, before THEY broke my heart?
Who is THEY? Everyone who was supposed to protect me from the start.
I was the little girl crying in her room, all alone, so confused, in trouble again,
broken and abused.
The bruises and tear stains fade as time goes by, I learned the art of concealment,
and refused to cry.
Now nothing can touch me, you can try if you dare, I'll just cast you off,
without a care.
No feelings left you see, THEY beat them out of me.
I feel nothing, it's sad, I agree, but at least now I'm free.

ROUTINE

Open your eyes and welcome to life,
A place where you are wrong, and you have to fight to be right.
Where routine is expected, and nothing else is excepted.
Routine can be hard when you're trying to survive the chaos every day,
Wishing you were normal, and the chaos in your head would just go away.
The routine we are forced to keep, has a way of suffocating me.
You cannot box up my creativity, it makes me want to explode and break free.

WRITER

I am a writer who doesn't write for recognition,
fortune or fame.
I write to eliminate all of my, pushed down,
burned into your soul, kind of pain.
The kind that you cover-up, pretending that it's
no longer there.
Until you are triggered, back sliding, bracing
yourself for the fall.
Hands on your head screaming, praying that
God will just take it all.
All of the pain, sorrow, and loss,
All of the anxiety, and complexity, that's stuck in
your mind.
Writing, bleeding on paper, trying to get it out,
before it takes me under,
one last time.

PATH

From the time we take our first breath, until our very last,
we are set upon a course in life, struggling to find the right path.
Our first cry of real sorrow, shattering our hearts like broken glass,
Hurt and confused we shy away from that path.
Guarded now, as one should be, planning my path so diligently.
I examined my life, and the paths that I chose, and decided to walk with the Lord,
For on his path the love just grows.

HEART and MIND

My heart screamed because it was tired of being alone,
My mind hushed it and covered it with stone.
The heart lays there silent, trusting the mind that knows best.
My mind is tired of the pain, it just wants to rest.
One day perhaps, I will set my heart free, but with all that I've experienced,
it's really not likely.

THINK OF ME?

I wonder if you ever think of me.
Do I ever cross your mind? Is there a certain memory, that replays constantly?
So, do you ever think of me, when you've laid awake at night?
When all is settled, and everything is quiet?
Do you ever wonder if I am ok, because I've gotten so good at hiding myself,
and pushing people away.
Do you ever wonder if I think about you?
I would like to say I don't, but then, that wouldn't be true.

NOT TODAY

I watched as my world fell apart around me, I just stood there,
staring at crumbled memories.
I waited for the pain, because that's how it's supposed to be,
But there was no pain, it was something much worse.
It was emptiness, hollowness, this was the beginning of a divorce.
The betrayal, the lies, and petty schemes,
Ignoring broken promises, and not wanting to look at the shattered dreams.
So, I stepped away, I shut myself down, I'm not strong enough to face this,
Not today anyway, not right now.

NOTHING

How is it possible that I feel nothing? I'm living
in a void, without any emotion.
I don't feel anything, he stripped me of
everything.
I allowed it, I take full responsibility.
I took on his demons, trying to ease his
suffering,
Now I'm just left with this nothingness, I
destroyed myself,
trying to save him.
I stayed to long in his world, and now I don't
know how to pull myself
from the darkness.
No love, no light, no hate, no spite, just nothing.

SECRETS

What dark secrets run through my blood?
What treasures lay buried deep in my soul,
that I know nothing about?
How do I fill a hole inside of me, where the
other half of my family should be?
Long midnight walks, Lond serious talks,
Speaking to a dad that no longer exists,
conversing with God about my brokenness.
Wanting to know why, or what, or who I am.

GUIDE ME

The sun sets, the night falls, the darkness beckons,
and the lonely will answer its call.
Up all night, can't sleep, wandering, searching,
digging through my life, just looking
for my truth, asking God, please shed some light.
I come to You, broken, abandoned, and abused. there
are scars on my soul, that people can't see.
My life has shattered into chaos, and only You can
set me free.
So, I'm asking for strength, for courage, for each
passing day,
In a world filled with hate, I ask You, to please
guide my way.

I QUESTION

I can't understand why anyone would ever choose to love me.
I've never considered myself lovable, I am damaged, I am broken,
I have survived a life that tried to kill me.
I have scars that run deep within, that I won't allow anyone to ever see.
You would sense the contradiction, where I want to be free, and at the same time,
I want you to hold me.
Are you strong enough to break through?
Can you tear down these walls?
But my question is, why would you ever want to?

LOST LOVER

I saw you. I didn't even have time to prepare. We were both standing,
in the same parking lot. Time stood still, and all I could do was stare.
Clouds were rolling in, and the smell of rain was thick.
But I didn't even notice, because my mind was transfixed.
My longing for you has never ceased, I've carried you with me like a disease.
I could not stand there, I had to get away.
I couldn't let you see me, we both know, I'd never be able to stay.
With the rain crashing down, I huddled inside my car,
letting the memories wash over me, leaving a new scar.
I watched as you drove out of the parking lot, out of my life, but not,
out of my heart.

I'M OUT

You tried to destroy my life with lies, knowing I could end you with the truth.
But, hey, okay. I'll play the villain in your make-believe world,
If it means I can break ties with you.
You're not going to let me go that easy, you like to watch me hurt,
you like to see me bleed.
You get off on the trauma you cause. What? You think I don't, see?
But there's something you need to learn about me.
You can't hold me down, I'm stronger than you think, I will get out,
I will heal me, I can deal with all this trauma, and now, PTSD.

BEAUTIFULLY BROKEN

I am beautifully broken; I need to get up and fix my crown.
I can't let my pieces lay on this cold hard ground.
I may be broken, but I am not weak.
You can see my strength, in my stance, and hear it when I speak.
I've had to grow stronger, in order to hold all of these pieces together.
But I've been doing it for so long now, they really feel light as a feather.
So, imagine how strong you would have to be, to hold a million pieces together,
in such a way, that no one would be able to see.

FREE FROM YOU

The words you say, cut me so deep.
You don't notice, you never see, the moments I hang my head and weep.
You want me to except you for who you are, but who you are is killing me.
I can feel my life drain, I can feel my spirit wane.
I'm pulling away, I just long to be free.
Free of pain, free from the cruel words, and uncertainty.
Free from the madness that comes with loving you.
Oh, and I have loved you, why else would I have stayed?
I have tried to help you understand your cruelty, and what you do to me,
but eventually I had to admit, you're one person that I can't save.

SOULMATE

When my mind is overwhelmed with chaos, and
my thoughts are spinning out of control,
You look at me, you touch me, and my body is
flooded with such amazing comfort,
All the way down to my soul.
I can feel the anxiety rushing out of me, as you
pull me into you.
You are the anchor that holds me steady, in the
middle of my storm, you are the beacon of light,
that I search for in the dead of night.
Soulmates, I never thought any of that was true,
Not until the day, I met you.

www.ingramcontent.com/pod-product-compliance
Lightning Source LLC
Chambersburg PA
CBHW051719130826
49812CB00034B/1250
9789357215978